Matthew Henson
& Robert Peary

Terry Barber

FAMOUS
FIRSTS
SERIES

Matthew Henson & Robert Peary is published by
Grass Roots Press, a division of Literacy Services of Canada Ltd.

PHONE 1–888–303–3213
WEBSITE www.literacyservices.com

ACKNOWLEDGEMENTS

We acknowledge the financial support of the Government of Canada through the Book Publishing Industry Development Program (BPIDP) for our publishing activities.

We acknowledge the support of
the Alberta Foundation for the Arts
for our publishing programs.

Editor: Dr. Pat Campbell
Image research: Dr. Pat Campbell
Book design: Lara Minja, Lime Design Inc.
Book layout: Andrée-Ann Thivierge, jellyfish design

Library and Archives Canada Cataloguing in Publication

Barber, Terry, date
        Matthew Henson & Robert Peary / Terry Barber.

(Famous Firsts series)
ISBN 978-1-894593-66-3

        1. Henson, Matthew Alexander, 1866-1955. 2. Peary, Robert E.
(Robert Edwin), 1856-1920. 3. Arctic regions--Discovery and exploration.
3. Readers for new literates. I. Title.

PE1126.N43B3646 2007   428.6'2   C2007-902786-5

Printed in Canada.

Contents

First men to reach the top of Everest.

First woman to fly
across the Atlantic Ocean.

First man to fly solo
across the Atlantic Ocean.

These people risk their lives to be first.

Risk-takers

Why do some people always have to
be first? They have to be first in line.
They have to be the first to own an
item. Some people will even risk their
lives to be first.

Robert Peary.

Risk-takers

It is 1892. Two men want to reach
the North Pole. They are willing to
risk their lives. One of the men is
black. His name is Matthew Henson.
The other man is white. His name is
Robert Peary. Both men live in the U.S.

Matthew
Henson.

Peary gets his degree from Bowdoin College.

Bowdoin College.

Robert Peary's Dream

Peary is born in 1856. At the age of six, he reads a book on Greenland. He dreams of going to the **Arctic**.

Peary goes to college. He gets his degree in 1877. After college, Peary joins the U.S. Navy.

Peary is an engineer in the U.S. Navy.

9

The Civil War ends slavery.

Matthew Henson

Henson is born in 1866. He is born after the Civil War. The Civil War ends slavery. But, black people still have fewer choices than white people. Black people have the worst jobs. They get the worst pay. And they get the worst education.

The Civil War goes from 1861 to 1865.

MARYLAND

UNITED STATES

Before the Civil War, slavery is legal in 15 states.

Matthew Henson

Maryland is a slave state. But, Henson's parents are not born into slavery. They are both born free. Henson's father is a **sharecropper.** The family is very poor. Henson is born in Maryland.

Like this man, Henson's father works in a tobacco field.

A one-room school for black children.

Matthew Henson

Henson's mother dies when he is seven. Henson is sent to live with his uncle. Henson goes to school for six years. He loves to hear stories about the sea. Henson gets restless. He leaves school to see the world.

At an early age, Henson moves with his family to Washington, D.C.

Henson walks to the port in Baltimore, Maryland.

Matthew Henson

Henson walks 40 miles (64 km) to reach a **port**. Henson finds work on a steam-ship. He works as a cabin boy. At sea, Henson learns to read maps. He learns to read the stars.

Henson sails to China, Japan, the Philippines, North Africa, Spain, France, and Russia.

Robert Peary.

Matthew Henson

Henson sails on ships for many years. Then he gets restless again. Henson leaves the sea. He moves from place to place. He works odd jobs. At the age of 18, Henson's life changes. He meets Robert Peary.

Henson meets Peary in 1887. Henson is Peary's assistant for 23 years.

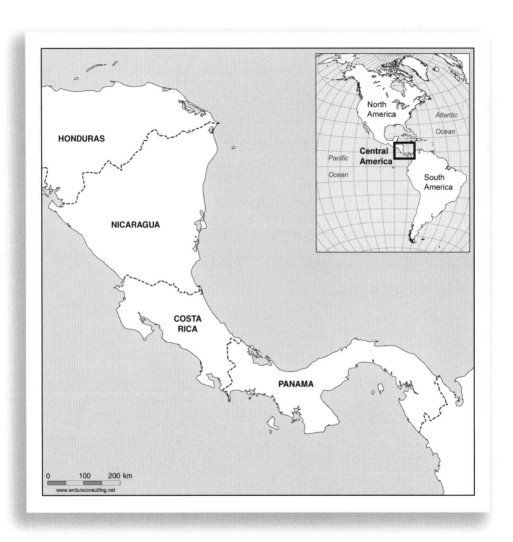

Peary explores Nicaragua, Central America.

Henson and Peary

The U.S. Navy wants Peary to explore Central America. Peary hires Henson to help him. They learn each other's strengths. Peary shares his dream with Henson. Peary wants to be the first man to reach the North Pole.

Henson and Peary survey the jungle in Nicaragua. They return to the U.S. in 1888.

Robert Peary.

Henson and Peary

Henson and Peary love to explore. They love adventure. They are also different. Peary lives to reach his goal. He thinks about the North Pole all the time. Henson is not like that. Henson lives more in the moment.

Matthew Henson.

Peary meets the Eskimos.

The Eskimos

In the 1890s, Peary and Henson make five trips to Greenland. They look for the best route to the North Pole. They meet **Eskimos**. Henson learns how to speak their language. Henson learns the Eskimo way of life.

Inuktitut is an Eskimo language.

Henson sits on a sledge.

The Eskimos

It is hard to live in the North. The Eskimos teach Henson how to survive. Henson learns how to build and drive a **sledge**. A sledge carries people and supplies. A team of dogs pulls a sledge across the snow and ice.

Henson improves the design of the sledge.

Eskimos building an igloo.

The Eskimos

By the 1890s, Eskimos had lived in
the North for thousands of years.
But, they had not seen the North
Pole. They think a devil lives near
the Pole. The Eskimos trust Henson.
They decide to travel with Henson
and Peary.

Henson sits with the Eskimos.

Peary finds it hard to walk without toes.

Bad Luck

Henson and Peary make three attempts to reach the North Pole. On their first attempt, they do not reach the North Pole. Peary loses nine toes to frostbite. But, they do not give up. They learn from their mistakes.

The *Roosevelt* is locked in the Arctic ice.

Bad Luck

Peary has a ship built for the second trip. It is called the *Roosevelt*. The ship is named after the U.S. President. It is built to travel in icy water. There are many storms during their second trip. Peary and Henson fail again.

Theodore Roosevelt is the U.S. President from 1901 to 1909.

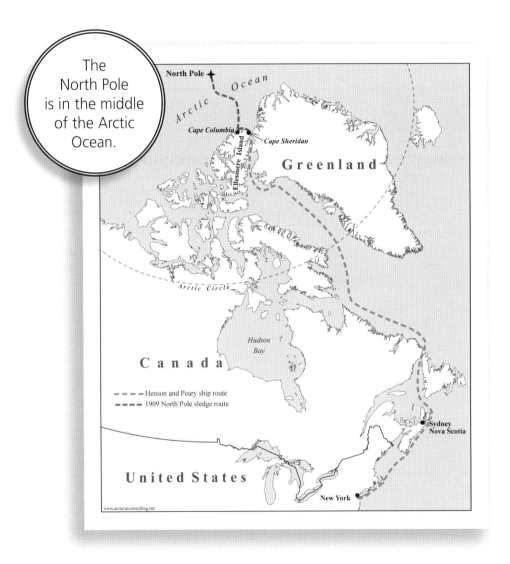

The
North Pole
is in the middle
of the Arctic
Ocean.

The 1908-1909 route to the North Pole.

Success at Last

It is July 6, 1908. Peary and Henson make their last attempt to reach the Pole. They sail from New York to Ellesmere Island. They reach the island on September 5. They prepare for the sledge trip to the North Pole.

The *Roosevelt* leaves New York.

A base camp.

Success at Last

It takes many months to get ready for the sledge trip. The men build base camps. The base camps are built between the island and the North Pole. The men store food and supplies at the base camps.

They take a stove to each camp.

A team crosses a lead of open water.

Success at Last

It is February 1908. Six teams of men start the sledge trip to the North Pole. The trip is 413 miles (665 km). They travel over ice. There are **leads** of open water. A fall into the icy water can be fatal.

Peary, Henson, and six Eskimos are on one team.

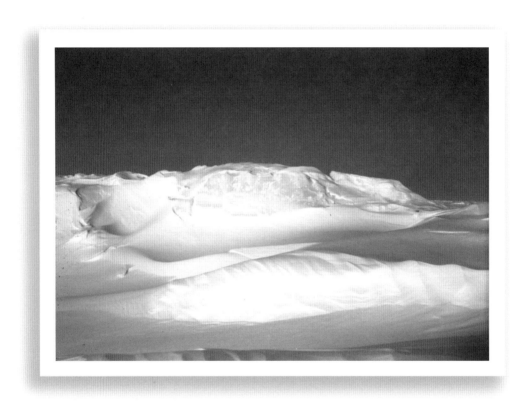

A ridge on the ocean.

Success at Last

The frozen ice is not flat. The ice moves and forms **ridges**. The ridges can form very quickly. They can form overnight. Ridges are piles of broken ice. They are 30 to 50 feet high. It is hard to travel over the ridges.

The team travels over a ridge.

Henson and Peary's team walk to the Pole.

Success at Last

It is April 1, 1909. Henson and Peary are 133 miles (214 km) from the Pole. Henson sets a hard **pace**. They walk 18 to 20 hours a day. They are cold, tired, and hungry. They keep going. They will not quit.

Peary and Henson stand by
the North Pole with three Eskimos.

Success at Last

On April 6, 1909, Henson and Peary reach the Pole. Their dream comes true. Henson would not have reached the Pole without Peary. Peary would not have reached the Pole without Henson. They gain fame by working as a team.

Henson and Peary return to the U.S. in the fall of 1909.

Glossary

Arctic: the area north of the Arctic circle.

Eskimo: a member of a group of Aboriginal people who live in the Arctic region. The term Inuit has replaced the word Eskimo.

lead: open water caused by a break in the ice.

pace: rate of speed in walking.

port: a place of shelter for ships.

ridge: a hill of ice on a large body of water.

sharecropper: a tenant farmer who gives a share of each crop as rent.

sledge: a strong, heavy sled.

Talking About the Book

What did you learn about Matthew Henson and Robert Peary?

In what ways are Henson and Peary similar and different?

What challenges did Henson face in his life?

What did you learn about the North Pole?

Why was it so hard to reach the North Pole?

In your opinion, why do some people want to be first?

Picture Credits

Front cover photos (center photo): © Library of Congress, Prints and Photographs Division, LC-USZ62-42993; (small photo): © The National Oceanic and Atmospheric Administration. Contents page (top right): © The Granger Collection, New York; (bottom left): © The National Oceanic and Atmospheric Administration; (bottom): © The Granger Collection, New York. Page 4 (bottom): © Royal Geographical Society; (left): © The Schlesinger Library, Radcliffe Institute, Harvard University; (right): © Lindbergh Picture Collection, Manuscripts and Archives, Yale University Library. Page 6: © Library of Congress, Prints and Photographs Division, LC-USZ62-120181. Page 7: © Explorers Club Research Collections. Page 8: © Library of Congress, Prints and Photographs Division, LC-USZ62-7486. Page 10: © Library of Congress, Prints and Photographs Division, LC-USZCN4-50. Page 13: © Library of Congress, Prints and Photographs Division, LC-USZ62-130504. Page 14: © Library of Congress, Prints and Photographs Division, LC-DIG-nclc-04341. Page 16: © Library of Congress, Prints and Photographs Division, LC-USZC2-3355. Page 18: © The National Oceanic and Atmospheric Administration. Page 20: Andreas (Andy) N Korsos, Professional Cartographer, Arcturus Consulting. Page 21: © istockphotos. Page 22: © The National Oceanic and Atmospheric Administration. Page 23: © The Granger Collection, New York. Page 24: © Library of Congress, Prints and Photographs Division, LC-USZC4-7505. Page 26: © LC-USZC4-7505, LC-USZ62-68223. Page 27: © Explorers Club Research Collections. Page 28: Private Collection/ The Stapleton Collection/ The Bridgeman Art Library. Page 29: Explorers Club Research Collections. Page 30: © Royal Geographical Society/ Bridgeman Art Library. Page 32: © CORBIS. Page 34: © Andreas (Andy) N Korsos, Professional Cartographer, Arcturus Consulting. Page 35: © Library of Congress, Prints and Photographs Division, LC-D4-39215. Page 36: © Private Collection/ The Stapleton Collection/ The Bridgeman Art Library. Page 38: © Library of Congress, Prints and Photographs Division, LC-USZ62-30643. Page 40: © The National Oceanic and Atmospheric Administration. Page 41: © Explorers Club Research Collections. Page 42: © Hulton Archive/Getty Images. Page 44: © National Archives, 542472.